Happy birthday Adam — Decembers 21
much love
jeannie x

Bank of Scotland, Earl Grey Street.

First Published October 2019

ALLAN WRIGHT PHOTOGRAPHIC

www.allanwrightphoto.com

Scotland

Images copyright © Allan Wright 2019

Introduction and poems copyright © Gerda Stevenson 2019

ISBN: 978-1-905683-92-5

Printed by Skleniartz, Poland

ACKNOWLEDGEMENTS

Design: Michael Melvin, Melvin Creative Ltd.

Associate editors: Carol Carr & Gerda Stevenson

The poems *Christmas Market* and *Scotland Celebrates 3-0 at Easter Road*
first published in Gerda Stevenson's poetry collections *If This Were Real*
(Smokestack Books, 2013) and in *Quines: Poems in tribute to women of Scotland*
(Luath Press, 2018), respectively, © Gerda Stevenson.

EDINBURGH

ALLAN WRIGHT   GERDA STEVENSON

ALLANWRIGHT
PHOTOGRAPHIC

Holyrood Park.

INTRODUCTION

WHEN ALLAN WRIGHT invited me to create a sequence of poems and a personal introduction for a book of his vibrant Edinburgh photographs, I was delighted to accept. Delighted, yet somewhat daunted – so many illustrious authors have written on the subject, not least Robert Fergusson. His glorious poem *Auld Reikie*, penned two hundred and fifty years ago, says it all. But Scotland's capital is my home city, and has always been close to my heart. The challenge was irresistible. This is a pivotal moment, in the wake of two recent referenda, as the United Kingdom's four nations jostle to realign their individual values and identities, not only in relation to one another, but within a European context.

Edinburgh has welcomed and beguiled me since childhood. I regularly took the bus 'into town' with my family, from the village where I was born and brought up, in the Pentland Hills – the *Hills of Home*, as Robert Louis Stevenson called them – just half an hour or so from Edinburgh's centre. This great city taught me to understand that being a Scot means I'm European. I learned this from visits throughout my childhood and teens to the Scottish National Gallery where Scotland's great artists are celebrated in the company of the Dutch, French, Spanish and Italian masters. This sense of being European deepened in adulthood, performing at Edinburgh's Royal Lyceum in Scots language translations of classics such as Edwin Morgan's version of Racine's *Phaedre*, and Liz Lochhead's adaptation of Molière's *Tartuffe*.

My earliest Edinburgh memory is of visiting the Museum of Childhood, on the Royal Mile, the first museum in the world dedicated to the history of childhood. I remember being thrilled and terrified in equal measure by a box that lit up with a drum roll when you put a coin into a slot, to reveal a gruesome guillotine scene from the French Revolution. The blade whizzed down onto the model of a wee man and chopped off his head which bounced into a basket. In another room, a poor child's doll made by a parent from an old boot saddened and unsettled me.

One gloomy December dusk, in my last year at high school, Edinburgh gave me first love. Christmas lights and street lamps loomed through the fog as I walked from the bus station down to Barony Street, where I entered a drafty close and climbed the stone stairs to a top flat. I braced my nerves to run the gauntlet of the landlady's judgmental stare before entering my boyfriend's bedsit. He was a student at Edinburgh College of Art, and had draped his room in Eastern silks, tea-lights glimmering in every corner.

Snow was falling when we went out onto the street hours later, having missed the last bus home. We walked back to the Pentlands together in the small hours, singing carols all the way.

The Edinburgh of my imagination is always a winter one, captured so vividly by Allan Wright in this book: a snowscape of iced rooftops, spires and bridges, the sheltering white shoulder of Salisbury Crags, with Arthur's Seat presiding sage-like over all.

After I left high school, I had a full-time job as a care worker. On the occasional Saturday off, I'd take a trip into town. My favourite haunt was a bookshop on George Street called *The Grail*, a honeycomb of rooms lined with books and hessian wallpaper. The floorboards creaked amiably under rush matting, and Bach or Mozart floated on the air. Deliciously moist walnut cake was served on wooden plates, and the aroma of coffee enveloped you like a comfort blanket – especially enticing when winter frost nipped the air. You could sit in an armchair munching cake and sipping coffee, reading books without buying them – no-one bothered you, which may be why *The Grail* had a relatively short life-span. I did make a couple of purchases – the complete works of Oscar Wilde, and a volume of Hans Andersen's stories. I have them on my shelves today, the dust jackets still bearing the shop's faded label.

Before I moved to Edinburgh, I'd spent a couple of years living in the Highlands, and, being a country girl, had wondered whether I might feel claustrophobic as a city-dweller. But I found myself very much at home. Edinburgh is designed on a human scale, mercifully spared the devastation of a motorway slicing through its heart. You can easily make your way on foot across the city centre, out to its nearest environs, including the seven hills around which Edinburgh is built – Castle Rock and Calton Hill, Holyrood Park's majestic Arthur's Seat and Salisbury Crags, Braid Hills, Blackford Hill, Corstorphine Hill, and Craiglockhart Hill, wonderful wild places to walk if you want to blow away the cobwebs and give your spirits an airing. Ideal terrain, too, for an actor to tramp in dogged rhythm while learning lines, a task I've always disliked, but made much more tolerable outdoors, especially when I'm high up with a good view to the North Sea.

I've worked in all of Edinburgh's fine theatres – each with its own distinctive backstage smell – including the old Traverse in the Grassmarket, as well as the new one in Cambridge Street. I came out of the Traverse recently, the first week of the city's annual Edinburgh International Festival and Fringe well underway. I'd been to see a new black comedy set during the Troubles in Northern Ireland, performed to a packed auditorium. I turned the corner, heading along Castle Terrace, and saw two homeless men settling in for the night under a duvet against the building in which the Traverse is housed – Saltire Court, the heart of Edinburgh's financial district. Luckily for the men, it was a clear, warm night, not typical of our capital.

The view from their open-air 'east windy, west-endy' sleeping quarters was the Castle, spectacularly illuminated above them. I paused for a moment, struck by such stark juxtapositions: Britain's colonial past still playing out in Scotland's renowned new writing theatre, and the old inequalities, described by Robert Louis Stevenson in the opening of his classic book *Edinburgh*, as present today as they were in his time. I was keenly reminded of my good fortune: to have lived in this uniquely beautiful city with my own roof over my head. In our current era of extreme tourism, the dark underbelly of the city is a story not often told – homeless communities existing cheek by jowl with the wealthy districts.

My own work as a writer and director has involved projects which have given voice to Edinburgh's marginalised communities. In preparation for writing a radio drama about homelessness, I spent several months in and around the city, researching with linchpin organisations such as The Rock Trust and Streetwork, as well as City of Edinburgh Council, interviewing homeless people and service providers. This process was a huge education for me, a stark reminder of the misinformation pedalled by the popular press about the disenfranchised among us.

And there's another, connected story, of Edinburgh citizens who were decanted from the city centre, and posted out to concrete suburbs such as Pilton, Muirhouse, Granton, Niddrie, Craigmillar and Wester Hailes, 'purpose built' at the time, yet without adequate infrastructure and community services. Author Alan Spence, our Edinburgh Makar, wrote a fine play on this theme – *Changed Days*, charting the social history of Edinburgh's inner-city slum areas from the late 1920s to the '80s, the script based on oral history material from former residents of the Old Town.

A heroine of this neglected Edinburgh reality was the indefatigable Helen Crummy, who set up the legendary and internationally acclaimed Craigmillar Festival Society. Helen tells the story herself in her remarkable book *Let the People Sing*. The CFS produced many publications, Helen involved in most of them, including *The Comprehensive Plan for Action*, 1976, acknowledged as a milestone in Community Planning.

In leafing through Allan Wright's feast of photographs, considering which might provide me with material for poems, I was delighted to find images of the Royal Botanic Garden's magnificent Temperate Palm House – the tallest traditional glass house in the British Isles, and one of my favourite locations. It was here that I directed a children's opera with composer Dee Isaacs, who leads the ground-breaking Music in the Community course at the University of Edinburgh.

Pupils from Leith Walk Primary School performed the work, along with the university's students and a small core of professional performers. Many of the children were from immigrant families – Polish, Iranian, Romanian, Russian, Pakistani, Indian. Half way through rehearsals, a Sudanese child refugee joined us, immediately welcomed into the fold by her classmates, most of whom had never been in a garden before, let alone such a world-class botanical one. It was a privilege to witness the joy they experienced during rehearsals and performance, in the freedom of such a beautiful space. This was a night-time promenade production. The children led their audience through the magically lit grounds and chain of glass houses, the Temperate Palm House our setting for the final scene. Their young voices, singing in harmony, ring in my memory with the clarity of glass.

Edinburgh means different things to many people, both residents and visitors alike. I love the city for reasons particular to my own experience: that malt-rich, fruity smell of the breweries in the Gorgie-Dalry area, where I lived with my husband when we first moved to Edinburgh; the pleasure of browsing and attending events at the Scottish Poetry Library – the only purpose-built, independent public poetry library in the world, founded by another Edinburgh heroine, poet Tessa Ransford; the thrill of walking through the same streets that Walter Scott's characters inhabited in his novel *The Heart of Midlothian*; the never-to-be-forgotten day when I gave birth to my son in the Elsie Inglis Memorial Maternity Hospital, overlooking Holyrood Park; the Meadows with their clouds of cherry blossom where I taught him to ride a bike.

I've relished both the collaborative process of making this book – responding to another artist's work in a different medium – and the way in which the project unexpectedly developed: I found myself writing additional poems about aspects of the city which Allan then went out to photograph. The journey towards finding a visual and poetic narrative became a dynamic process of creative exchange.

My Edinburgh won't be your Edinburgh any more than yours will be mine. But here is Allan Wright's Edinburgh, my response to it, and, in turn, his response to mine – the interaction of two perspectives, adding, we hope, to the debate about Scotland's on-going story; our tribute to one of the world's great capital cities.

GERDA STEVENSON, 2019.

Winter, North Bridge, Salisbury Crags and Arthur's Seat.

SLEEPING LION

When the moon is full I purr to her.
I used to blether, through the clear nights,
chronicles of my long life,
since glaciers ground their stately way
from West to East, and lava spilled.
We are watchers, she and I: we alone know
who buried those seventeen
dolls' coffins unearthed at my flanks;
we've seen a forest grow and die,
a palace, a parliament rise at my foothills
under the wax and wane of her silver eye;
but these days, I, so old, replete with tales,
and so familiar with her steady gaze,
no longer need to share the past
or changing ways of here and now
with words – when I have her full attention
on those high, fair nights, the sharing is barely
a murmur; a purr will suffice.

Note: *Almost two hundred years ago, a group of boys, hunting for rabbits on Arthur's Seat, unearthed seventeen miniature coffins, each containing an intricately carved human figure. The origin of these mysterious objects is uncertain, but they are more or less contemporary with the trial of Burke and Hare, the infamous murderers, who provided Edinburgh anatomist, Dr Robert Knox, with seventeen dead bodies for dissection. Only eight of the coffins have survived intact. These can be seen in Edinburgh's National Museum of Scotland.*

Moonrise over Arthur's Seat from Blackford Hill.

Eco landscaping, Scottish Parliament, Holyrood.

Scott Monument & autumnal Acer leaves, Princes Street Gardens.

Precipitous Moroccan mind benders, Festival Fringe, High Street.

Festival Fringe street theatre, High Street.

CAMERA OBSCURA

Closing time in the twilit winter half-light,
the sky washed after rain, footfalls
of another thronging day at last dissolved,
and my walls slumber in neon glow;
by day I'm all eyes, mistress of illusion:
I filter visions to tantalise the lens and retina,
and lay before a thousand avid irises a living record
of the capital's life, a pinpoint of concentric circles,
its ripples, as Geddes marked, pulsing out
through Scotland, to Europe and the world.

Note: *Patrick Geddes, Scottish biologist, sociologist, geographer, philanthropist and pioneering town planner, purchased the Camera Obscura building in 1892, with a view to developing it as 'a place of outlook and a museum-type as a key to a better understanding of Edinburgh and its region, but also to help people get a clear idea of its relation to the world at large'.*

Camera Obscura and Scotch Whisky Heritage Centre, Castlehill.

Royal Mile Tavern, High Street.

Deacon Brodie's Tavern, Lawnmarket.

Street theatre artist, Festival Fringe, St Giles Cathedral.

BURLESQUE HUMAN STATUE

Who knows the gender
of this fantoush flouter,
this merry bender
of douce Edinburgh rules?
And who cares! It's Festival time –
(though a few more women
on the capital's pedestals
wouldn't go amiss,
and this one's certainly
taking the piss!);
stock-still on a soapbox,
she's her own master,
blows her own whistle,
pulls her own strings:
a sudden tug
and her crinoline flips
up to her oxters – a sunlit airing
of suspenders, knickers and thighs;
and those silk-stockinged legs
(mess with them at your peril!),
swords daubed on knee-cap and shin,
they're spoiling for a duel.
If buildings could smile, I'd say
St. Giles is leaning that way,
at sight of this white-wigged
fright of an upstart,
this unholy sprite.

Homeless, Royal Mile.

Balmoral Hotel clock-tower and pillars of the National Monument of Scotland, Calton Hill.

NO FIXED ABODE

Light soars in arched ranks
from church windows above them –
the graveyard's living dead,
lost to the lower depths
of life's dark margins;
in black catacombs below
the West End's thronging shoppers,
their fitful breath condenses
on the frosted night,
a desperate congregation
gathered around the litter
of obliteration, while the city's choirs
praise a saviour's love.

St John's Church, West End of Princes Street.

David Hume, Lawnmarket.

St Giles Cathedral.

Debating chamber of the Scottish Parliament, Holyrood.

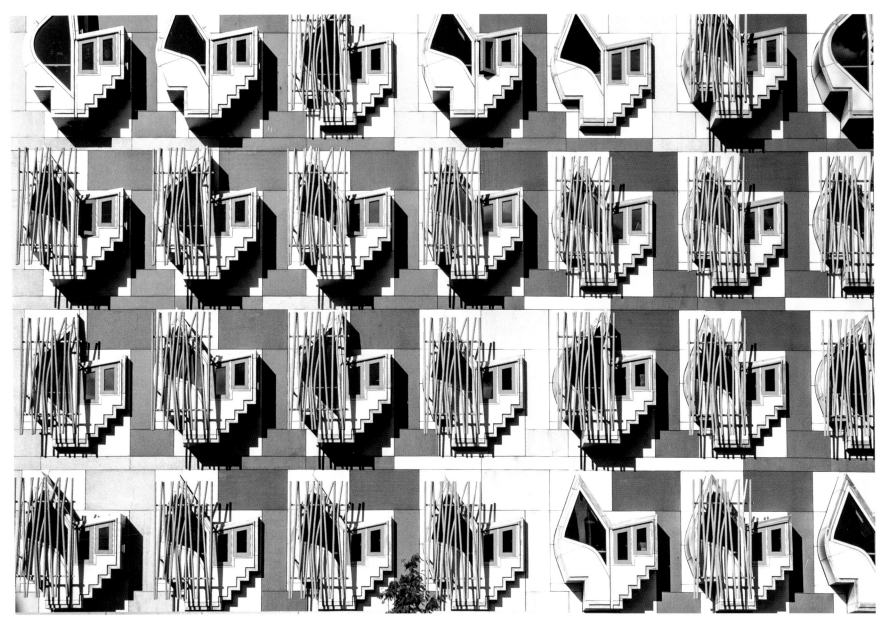

Casement windows of the MSP offices, Scottish Parliament, Holyrood.

HOLYROOD

The second Scottish Parliament.

Weel, here I am, her offspring, cooryin in –
ower three hunner year sin mither wis shut doon
bi a parcel of rogues linin their pooches, content
tae lat Scotland and maist o its fowk –
the yins wi nae vote – be bocht and sold
for a haunfu o glisterin Westminster gold.

But hey-ho, there ye go – despite some
amang the body politic takkin the humph
at ma conception (a rare European brew!)
and girnin at the cost o ma troublit birth –
I'm findin ma feet on the nation's map,
aheid o the gemm wi three leids on ma tongue,
and still in ma teens!

Sae, gie ma youthheid a thocht whan ye cast yer een
ower ma lanky anatomy, no yet autonomous,
but ilka pairt growin intae its richtfu place:
a playfu jigsaw bi day, a honeycomb o amber licht
come daurk, ma roof a fleet o boats
stowed wi guid wark, sailin frae nicht's hairt
intae a bricht dawn.

Dusk, Scottish Parliament, Holyrood.

Red blazers at Fettes College.

Cosmic landscape art by Charles Jenks, Gallery of Modern Art, Belford Road.

UNFINISHED BUSINESS

The National Monument of Scotland

Once dubbed a disgrace,
a shame, a carbuncle, a blight
on the capital's enlightened face,
it seems that's all forgotten now:
humiliated, I'm rehabilitated,
part of the furniture,
an incomplete masterpiece,
(through lack of expenditure) –
dare I say, an apt emblem
for Scotland today?

My purpose is twofold, or so we're told –
memorial to past heroes, and incentive to the bold
in future times; I'm not *quite* the Parthenon,
but come rain, hail or less likely shine,
here in Auld Reekie, our Athens of the North,
in the land of the old Caledonian pine,
my great credential is to offer potential;
meanwhile the status quo will do –
I'm already a landmark, almost an icon,
and doesn't history tell, as the years accrue,
we're content to make do?

Pillars of the National Monument of Scotland, Calton Hill.

Ainslie Place, New Town.

Doune Terrace, Stockbridge, New Town.

Hibernian Football Club, Easter Road.

SCOTLAND CELEBRATES 3-0 AT EASTER ROAD

Scotland v England, Saturday, 7th May, 1881, Easter Road, Edinburgh – the first recorded women's international football match, Scotland's winning team wearing knickerbockers, boots, red stockings and belts in the style of the Rational Dress movement.

The wind was against us – but wasn't it ever?
We had all to play for, and nothing to lose;
we kicked off with gusto, no matter the weather,
two thousand, the crowd, their jeers couldn't bruise
our spirits; red stockings and belts a kindling flicker
across the turf, then flashes of fire, flames fanned
by self-belief, we were bonded as one, slicker
than our English sisters, that day; we spanned
the field, every inch covered, Ethel hardly required
in goal – but when her moment came, oh, the spring
in her fearless lunge to save - the whole team fired!
We surge forward, and hear someone sing,
a lone voice, at first, *Daughters of Freedom Arise*,
then more and more: *Yield not the battle till ye have won!* –
our striker takes possession, her mind on the prize,
Lily St. Clair, talk about flair! – a meteor cast from the sun –
dancing and dodging, she blazes to the box, and bends
the ball in – a goal for Scotland! We weep and cheer,
Scotia's Eleven makes history, sends
a message to the world: have no doubt, we are here,
scaling the heights, new horizons in our sights
and the ball is rolling for women's rights.

Wardrop's Court, off Lawnmarket, Old Town.

Playground, Pilton.

Helen Crummy Memorial sculpture by Tim Chalk, Craigmillar.

THE BALLAD OF CRAIGMILLAR

Helen Crummy MBE, LLD, 1920-2011, Edinburgh; living in Craigmillar, one of the poorest areas on Edinburgh's outskirts, she improved the lives of its people and her own family, through artistic activity, founding the Craigmillar Festival Society, which gained international acclaim.

Embro Toon's got a braw new goon
so we're bombed oot, sent tae settle doon
on its concrete hem – the killer gemm
o 'us an them', auld as time, tick-tock, tick-tock,
in cauld Craigmillar o the high, bare rock.

The city faithers cannae stand the look
o folk like us stravaigin their streets
when the fancy elites fly in tae tak seats
in their concert halls – so they sweep us up
an tip us intae boxes like trash in the sticks,
suburban hicks; the mould on the waas
maks ye sick; nae wark, nae nuthin,
hee-haw tae dae, nae need fur a clock
in dreich Craigmillar o the high, bare rock.

Oh, they gied us a bus route, wi a map,
grand tae peruse, but whit's the use
when ye huvnae the coins
fur a hurl intae toon, tae see the place
in its starry new goon, niver mind
the crispy notes wi the queen's soor face
ye'd need tae cough up in the race
tae get a space tae see Pavarotti?
Couldnae happen tae us, let's be honest, Jock,
frae grotty Craigmillar o the high, bare rock.

Weel, that's whit we thought – aye, until...
a wumman tells the Heidie doon at the schuil
her son wants tae learn the violin –
no the fiddle, ken, the classical hing –
'Never!' says he, 'These kids cannae count!'
But she's got thick skin, decides tae mount
a big campaign – respect tae the wumman,
she's got some brain, an the guts tae keep gaun,
come sun, come rain; it's aa systems go,
we're gonnae pit oan a show, dae it oorsel,
it's ma job tae ring the startin bell –
a 'promenade' – ding! ding! stop the blether,
gaither thegither! And that's no aa,
she's got mair plans tae get us a haa,
a library, the stuff we need 'tae feed oor saul' –
that's whit she says – as weel's oor belly;
she gets on the phone, gies a call
tae the telly, the news, an folk are comin here –
they cannae refuse! – frae Embro Toon,
aa the airts, their jinin in,
an her laddie's learnin the violin;
aye, we're on the move, an we're takkin stock,
in oor Craigmillar o the high, bare rock.

Note: *Craigmillar derives from Creag Maol Ard, which means the high, bare rock,*
originally named at a time when Gaelic was spoken throughout most of Scotland.

Helen Crummy Memorial sculpture by Tim Chalk, Craigmillar.

Castle and residences by Kilgraston Road, Marchmont, from Blackford Hill.

View from Calton Hill.

John Knox, St. Giles Cathedral.

John Knox House, Canongate.

HENRY DUNDAS, 1ST VISCOUNT MELVILLE

1742-1811, Edinburgh; the most influential politician in the British government of his time: Home Secretary, War Secretary, Chief Secretary for India, and First Lord of the Admiralty, arguably more powerful than his friend Prime Minister William Pitt the Younger.

You may bleat your outrage,

but it's beneath me, and won't take its toll.

I'm above all that, solid as my column,

and mighty as the Empire I strove to build –

I'm a Scot, after all, and can thole time's weather.

Granted, we lost America under my watch,

but my sights were always high enough

to view the long game. Tell me this:

did your forebears complain

when my single-word amendment to the Bill

prolonged the slave trade's gravy train?

They were content, I think, to sup with me

the profits for another generation.

I got things done – reined Ireland in,

took India, rolled out the penal colony

in Botany Bay, corralled South Africa,

my favourite child, into the fold:

Hear the ring of a global brand:

Melvillle, Dundas from land to land!

The winds of change might blow me down,

but I've earned the heft of every block

you've built to laud me on this plinth.

Note: *Dundas supported Wilberforce's Bill in the British parliament to abolish slave trading, but added the word 'gradually' as an amendment, which anaesthetised the Bill, allowing the capturing and trading of a further half million slaves for another generation.*

The Melville Monument, St Andrew Square.

Rear of Ramsay Garden apartments, Castlegate, Royal Mile.

Hogmanay projections, General Registrar House, Princes Street.

Forth Bridge.

The Forth Bridges: Rail, Road and the Queensferry Crossing.

BRIDGE

Always a risk, reaching out
across the element that could drown you,
into the unknown, the mystifying North,
where language changes, and mountains rise
from thick fog like sudden sentinels
to challenge your mapping skills;
a leap of faith, like the one the pilgrims took
when they first set out to meet the veiled shore
sailing to the holy place, long before
steel ropes balanced a new road
in the bright air.

Note: *In the 11th century, Queen Margaret established a ferry across the Firth of Forth for pilgrims travelling to St Andrews in Fife.*

The now retired Forth Road Bridge.

Dean Village and the Water of Leith.

Gable end mural, North Junction Street, Leith.

Forth Ports Authority, formerly the old pumping station at Prince of Wales Dry Dock, Leith.

Royal Yacht Britannia, Ocean Terminal, Leith.

LEITH

Independent state, that's me!
Ma ain history maks me staun oot
frae you, smairt Embro,
wi yer heich opeenion o yersel.
I've aye been the talk o The Walk –
the braw sister toon, wi ma Citadel
and port, and I've hud the croon:
King Jamie the Saxt on oor side
in the Leith-Embro Wars
when we fair packed a punch
at yer muckle castle waas!
Sae tak tent – mind oan:
I'm ma ain witness:
dinnae speak fur Leith, Embro –
I'm no your business!

Note: *After the abdication of Mary Queen of Scots, civil war broke out from 1571-1573, a period known as the Wars between Leith and Edinburgh. Troops fighting for Mary's son, James the Sixth of Scotland (Jamie the Saxt), against his mother's supporters in Edinburgh Castle, based themselves in Leith.*

Leith Waterfront.

Cramond.

Dusk, South Queensferry High Sreet.

Craigmillar Castle.

SEVEN HAIKU FOR CRAIGMILLAR CASTLE

Gorse in summer sun,
fierce and sharp as history,
on the high, bare rock:

Craigmillar, succour
to Mary Queen of Scots when
Rizzio bled to death;

a haven of peace
in the lonely, blood-soaked wake
of her first child's birth.

Yet walls are neutral:
host to a secret pact made
to kill her husband;

shelter for dark trees,
immortal yews planted there
in Mary's honour,

a rooted duo
she knew as saplings within
the ancient courtyard;

today their branches
form an arc under blue sky,
holding memory.

Portobello Beach.

Musselburgh Promenade.

Salisbury Crags and city.

IN LABOUR

at Elsie Inglis Memorial Maternity Hospital, Abbeyhill.

I look out across Holyrood Park
from a square of hospital window
between each contraction's burning arc,
and crave yellow hawkweed, wet moss on stone,
that burst of sweet green on the tongue
when my teeth strip a grass stalk;
I know exactly where they grow,
as I lie, immobilised, wired to bleeping machines,
and haul them from their roots into the room,
draw their scent into my lungs
as your head crowns, then shoulders,
and for the first time your eyes,
blue as sky over the North Sea,
meet mine.

Water of Leith, Stockbridge.

The Colonies, Stockbridge.

TEMPERATE PALM HOUSE

Overture or grand finale –
I'm a resting place,
a transcendental symmetry
of sandstone, iron, glass and light,
a sanctuary guaranteed to slacken pace,
my climate clement at summer's height
or in deep midwinter, when the city's trees
scroll their nakedness across the sky;

stroll through this garden's chain of houses –
the world's varied climes held in glass:
cactus spines from arid desert lands,
waterfalls tumbling into fern-frothed groves,
rainforest lily pads wider than soup plates,
air humid as giants' breath;
I'll be there, a temperate prelude
or quiet coda, my perennial palms
fanning their fingers to the light.

Interior of Temperate Palm House, Royal Botanic Garden.

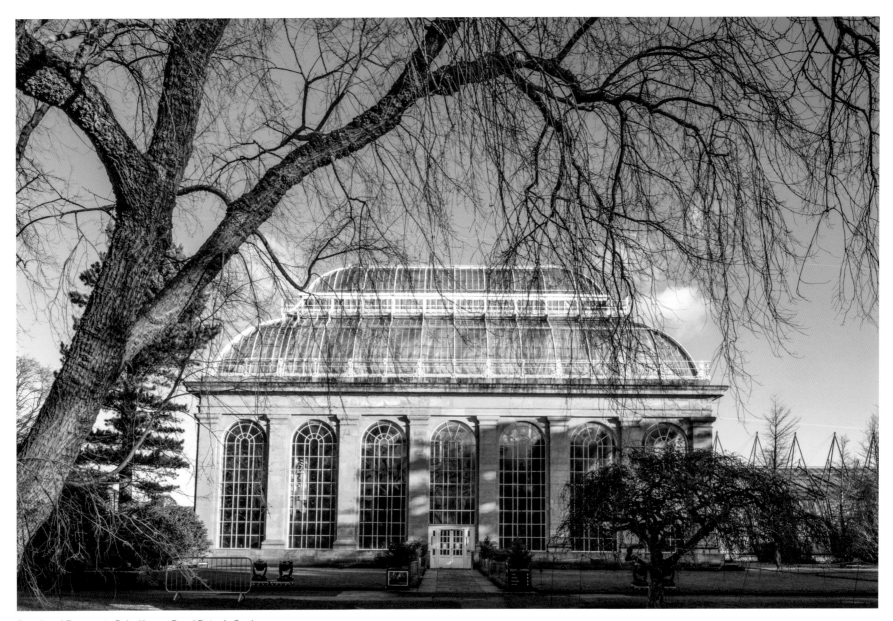

Exterior of Temperate Palm House, Royal Botanic Garden.

The National Monument of Scotland on Calton Hill, and Mossmorran gas plant, Fife.

FIDDLER IN THE CLOSE

On the terrace above Victoria Street,
grace notes stitch the air.
Like Ariadne's thread,
they lead me through a labyrinth,
tracking the ballad to its source.
I round the corner;
a stone lintel daubed 'Anon...'
heralds a presence below me
in the nook of a winding stairwell:
is she real, this candle-lit damsel
queen of fiddle in a velvet gown, perched
on a ledge above steps that might
draw me down to an underworld?
The passer-by ahead seems oblivious
to the vision that has stopped my heart
in this graffiti-splattered smoker's tryst,
scattered with fag-ends.
Her bow pauses on its upward sweep
and she nods her thanks as I offer mine –
a handful of clinking coins at her feet –
for a moment of unbidden alchemy.

Stairwell between Victoria Terrace and Victoria Street.

Victoria Street or West Bow, Old Town.

Greyfriar's Bobby.

St Margaret's Loch, and St Anthony's Chapel, Holyrood Park.

OH, WALY, WALY – THE AULD SANG

Noo Arthur's Seat shall be my bed,
No sheets shall e'er be pressed by me,
Saint Anton's Well shall be my drink,
Since my fause love's forsaken me.
                    An old Scots ballad.

Yon's whaur she drank at Saint Anton's Well,

the lass in a cramasie goon,

her fause love gane, a daith knell,

the trusty aik she'd leaned against,

his airms like brainches windit roon

her middle smaa; oh, he was aa her hame

in the lichtsome days afore his bairn

wis rootit in her wame;

the tears doon-faa, doon-faa.

She lookit oot, aa her lane,

her een on the daurk, faur faem

o the braid sea, whaur sailors prayed

at the howpfu sicht o Anton's waas,

thair braw stane, yon haly bield

that coudnae gie her ease.

Whaur is she noo, the lass in the sang,

her banes lang buiriet, lang, lang?

The daffin birds on the glisterin loch

fidderin there on whinnerin wings,

hae nae care but their ain sang,

the wheep o thair caa as they soar and faa

in the skimmer o licht – nae care ava.

Note: *It is thought that St Anthony's Chapel was intended to be a religious beacon, clearly visible to pilgrims and sailors as they sailed from and into the Firth of Forth. St Anthony is the patron saint of safe travel.*

Whitehorse Close, Holyrood, Royal Mile.

The Tolbooth, Canongate.

TURKISH RONDO

I thread my way through festival crowds
along Middle Meadow Walk, its braid
of global colours in full annual swing.
The old lion's head of Arthur's Seat
suns itself above us all, and from a circus tent
Mozart's Turkish Rondo percusses the muffled air,
a crazy clown tempo – even the bunting
is on the case, a wild chase on the wind's tail;
and suddenly it's visceral, this missing you,
that rondo you played when I was born,
how you made my whole body laugh
as a bairn, the way your Chico Marx fingers
teased the keys – Debussy's Cake Walk –
and that time we cheered in New York
for the sheer joy of Eubie Blake,
when a tap-dancing man wowed
the whole theatre to its feet, the pulse
of our connected lives in every beat.

Festival marquee, The Meadows.

Holyrood Palace.

AUOB Independence March, Radical Road, Salisbury Crags, Holyrood.

Family life, High Street.

Edinburgh Central Mosque, Potterrow.

EDINBURGH CASTLE

If iver there wis a castle that cried *Gie's peace!*
it's me. See the fechts I've tholed, the stooshies, the wars,
naethin but endless bluid and glaur
fur hunners o years – I'm the place maist attackit
in the hale o these isles, ma waas hackit,
and brunt, till ilka dunt hus duin in ma heid:
cannons, claymores, sgian dubhs, the Military Tattoo
juist gie me the blues. Whan the Wan o'Clock Gun
gaes aff ilka day, I'm a mess fur oors – I pray
at nicht it'll choke and brak doon, gie me
and the folk o Embro toon a rest frae the clatter,
no tae mention the fireworks – sic a blatter –
come festival time, they're the lest strae!
Oh, *Gie's peace!* is aa I huv tae say –
Gie's peace!

Note: *Edinburgh Castle is the most besieged place in the British Isles, and one of the most attacked in the world.*

Edinburgh Military Tattoo, 2019.

Massed pipe band, Military Tattoo.

Street theatre artist, High Street, Festival Fringe.

Early crocuses, The Meadows.

Thoroughfare and recreation, The Meadows.

USHER HALL, 3AM

The music box is closed,
silence locked in;
the crushed velvet pile
released from pressure adjusts
imperceptibly to plush
once more; the auditorium's air
settles itself, free of breath.

Long after the last footsteps have percussed
away over the cobbles, put your ear
to the stone façade in the heart of night –
will you hear a veiled wail from Shankar's sitar,
or a fragment of Callas embedded there –
sonic fossils from a century's atomised sound?

Usher Hall.

Festival Fringe brollies, St Giles Cathedral.

Detail of restored Ross Fountain, Princes Street Gardens.

Lloyds Banking Group Scottish Headquarters, the Mound.

Castle from rounded gable of St Cuthbert's Church, Princes Street Gardens.

STATUE OF A SOUTH AFRICAN WOMAN AND CHILD

by sculptor Anne Davidson, commissioned by the city of Edinburgh District Council to honour all those killed or imprisoned in South Africa for their stand against apartheid, unveiled in 1986.

What does she see, this woman
from a township far away, placed here
with her child in Scotland's capital,
fixed at street level, no pedestal,
smeared with lipstick by some joker,
making her eyes appear to bleed?
Is that what she sees – blood –
the flood of it, from Sharpeville and Nyanga,
washing in waves out to the Atlantic,
all the way to the North Sea and into Leith,
its crimson tinge lapping at Britannia's hull,
the floating palace, global ambassador, that sailed
with fanfare one sunlit morning into Table Bay,
taking our Queen to shake Mandela's hand,
her crown jewels' Cape diamonds mined
in the currency of blood?

South African Woman & Child, Lothian Road.

Muirhouse.

Prince Regent Street, Leith.

Advocate's Close, Royal Mile.

Silent swish of Edinburgh Tram, Princes Street.

CHRISTMAS MARKET

Arms linked, eyes locked,
wreathed in each other's breath,
they sip mulled wine and kiss.

Is their love new, keen as the tang
of lemon rind, or old and warm
as cinnamon and cloves?
Whatever the vintage, they're held
in its circle tonight, anonymous
within the crowd's geometry, still hub
among the stalls' kaleidoscope;
their bodies blend with intimate ease,
grey heads haloed by Ferris wheel neon,
oblivious to the caged cargoes
that shriek thrilled terror
into the Season of Love.

Winter Wonderland, Princes Street Gardens.

The Mound skyline and Princes Street Gardens.

Princes Street Gardens strollers.

AFTERMATH ON THE MEADOWS

Oh, the early morning stolen time
before the city wakes; the low,
slanted light as mist rises
and summer lets go –
crowds dispersed, stalls
and big tops stowed away,
only trees left for shelter;
stand under their kindling canopy,
reclaim the space on that fleeting cusp
when sap's invisible flow stills
below cloak of bark;
inhale the damp tang
as leaves release their hold
and wheel to earth
on the season's turn.

Autumnal avenue, The Meadows.

SCOTS GLOSSARY

aa	all
aa her lane	all on her own
afore	before
aheid	ahead
aik	oak
ain	own
airms	arms
airts	places
amang	among
attackit	attacked
Auld Reikie/Reekie	Edinburgh
ava	at all
aye	always
bairn	child
banes	bones
bi	by
bield	nest
blether	chat, converse
bluid	blood
braid	broad
brainches	branches
bocht	bought
brak	break
braw	fine, handsome, very good
bricht	bright
brunt	burnt
buiriet	buried
caa	call
cannae	can't
cauld	cold
claymore	a large sword
cooryin	nestling
couldnae	couldn't
cramasie	crimson
croon	crown
daffin	playing
daith	death
daurk	dark
dinnae	don't
doon	down
doon-faa	fall down
douce	respectable
duin	done
dunt	a heavy blow
een	eyes
Embro	Edinburgh
faem	foam
fair	certainly
faither	father
fantoush	fancy, stylish
faur	far
fause	false
fecht	fight
fidderin	fluttering
firewarks	fireworks
fowk	folk/people
frae	from
fur	for
gaes aff	goes off
gaither thegither	gather together
gane	gone
gaun tae	going to
gemm	game
gie	give
Gie's peace!	Give us peace!
girnin	moaning
glaur	muck, dirt
glisterin	glittering
gonnae	going to
goon	gown
guid	good
haa	hall
hackit	hacked
hae/huv	have
hairt	heart
hale	whole
haly	holy
haunfu	handful
hee-haw	nothing at all
heich	high
heid	head

hing	thing (also hang)	**oors**	hours (also ours)	**takkin the humph**	taking offence
howpfu	hopeful	**oorsel**	ourselves	**tak tent**	take care, attend to
hunners	hundreds	**oot**	out	**thair**	their
hurl	ride	**opeenion**	opinion	**thocht**	thought
hus	has	**ower**	over	**thole**	to put up with, endure
huvnae	haven't	**pairt**	part	**toon**	town
ilka	every	**pit oan**	put on	**troublit**	troubled
iver	ever	**playfu**	playful	**waas**	walls
jinin	joining	**pooches**	pockets	**waly**	an exclamation of sorrow
lang	long	**rootit**	rooted	**wame**	womb
lat	let	**sang**	song	**wark**	work
lest	last	**saxt**	sixth	**weel**	well
leid	language	**schuil**	school	**whan**	when
licht	light	**sgian dubh**	a ceremonial dagger (Gaelic)	**whaur**	where
lichtsome	light-hearted, delightful	**sic a blatter**	such a racket	**wheep**	a sharp cry or whistle
ma	my	**sicht**	sight	**whinner**	to whizz or whistle through the air
mak	make	**sin**	since		
Makar	poet (often a laureate)	**skimmer**	flicker	**wi**	with
mair	more	**smaa**	small	**windit**	wound around
maist	most	**smairt**	smart	**wis**	was
mind oan	think about, remember	**soor**	sour	**wumman**	woman
mither	mother	**stane**	stone	**ye'd**	you'd
naethin	nothing	**staun**	stand	**yin**	one
nicht	night	**stooshie**	fuss, skirmish	**yon**	that, those, yonder
niver	never	**strae**	straw	**youthheid**	adolescence
no	not	**stravaigin**	roaming		
noo	now	**tae**	to		

AFTERWORD **ALLAN WRIGHT**

I HAVE DERIVED a rewarding and novel sense of fellowship in creating this book. My initial concept was to produce a comparatively modest format, aimed at the photographically conscious visitor. By good fortune however, engaging Gerda Stevenson as co-author, and giving free rein to Carol Carr as associate editor, the scope and spirit of the work has widened and deepened. I hope therefore it has proved thought provoking at the very least, to those who have leafed through its pages.

The poetry collection featured in this book has, to my mind, interacted with my images to help penetrate the veneer that tends to dominate the city. All those prestigious castings and fine masonry may have collectively created one of Europe's most beautiful cities, but there were struggles in its making, and so often a human price was paid.

The majority of images featured here are quite recent, but I have included a small selection of my favourites that are much older. I enjoy working spontaneously taking a fluid approach, seeking subjects driven by the graphic strength of lines and ambient light. In a city such as Edinburgh the opportunities are boundless.